THE
BODY,
A TREE

THE BODY, A TREE

AMY MacLENNAN

MoonPathPress

Copyright © 2016 Amy MacLennan

Poetry

ISBN 978-1-936657-22-3

Cover art 'She Hangs Lanterns in the Night Sky'
by Beverly Ash Gilbert 2013
www.BeverlyAshGilbert.com

Author photo by Jenny Graham

Design by Tonya Namura using Frente (display) and Perpetua (text)

MoonPath Press is dedicated to publishing
the finest poets of the U.S. Pacific Northwest

MoonPath Press
PO Box 1808
Kingston, WA 98346

MoonPathPress@gmail.com

http://MoonPathPress.com

Acknowledgments

Many of these poems have appeared in the chapbooks:

The Fragile Day: Spire Press, 2011
Weathering: Uttered Chaos Press, 2012

Grateful acknowledgment to the editors of the following journals, anthologies, and online magazines, where these poems or earlier versions of them first appeared:

Against Rape: "It Takes a Few Days"

Cascadia Review: "Early Frost This Year," "Insomnia," "Painting the Room I Now Use for Guests," and "The Daylight is Huge"

Connotation Press: An Online Artifact: "On Living 366 Miles Apart"

Eating Her Wedding Dress: A Collection of Clothing Poems (Ragged Sky Press, 2009): "Lures"

Fieralingue – Health & Illness Anthology: "Fissures"

Hayden's Ferry Review: "The Drain"

jmww: "Garlic"

The Liberal Media Made Me Do It: Poetic Responses to NPR & PBS Stories (Nine Toes Press, 2014): "Thinning"

Linebreak: "Telegram"

The Literary Bohemian: "Up"

Myrrh, Mothwing, Smoke: Erotic Poems (Tupelo Press, 2013): "New"

The Oregonian: "Under"

Painted Bride Quarterly: "Between Two Ranges"

The Pedestal Magazine: "Kintsukuroi"

Poet's Market 2015: "Lusting"

qarrtsiluni: "Looking for an Oracle"

San Luis Obispo Poetry Festival Anthology: "Ritual"

The Sand Hill Review: "We Talk of the Dead" and "I Close My Eyes When I Listen to Poetry"

Scythe: "Miramar"

Slant: "Murmur" (previously titled "What the Heart Dictates")

The Smoking Poet: "If You Write a Love Letter to Disappointment" and "Green Olives with Medjool Dates"

Tattoo Highway: "Purity"

Tattoosday: "Heat and Hunger"

Turn (Uttered Chaos Press, 2013): "November, Late" and "Turn"

Weave: "Awake, Midnight"

Windfall: A Journal of Place: "Summer in Ashland"

Tupelo Press 30/30 Project, February 2014: "How You," "Before You Kissed Me," "Poem Written on Valentine's Day," "The Day We Both Call In," "A Kiss on the Cheek," "Heat and Hunger," and "Ritual"

"November, Late" was reprinted in *Forgetting Home: Poems About Alzheimer's* (Barefoot Muse Press Press, 2013); "Lures" was reprinted in *Pearl*; "I Close My Eyes When I Listen to Poetry" was reprinted in *First Water: Best of Pirene's Fountain* (Glass Lyre Press, 2013); "New" was reprinted in *Lummox*; "Telegram," "Painting the Room I Now Use for Guests," and "Looking for an Oracle" were reprinted in *The Poetry Storehouse*; "The Drain" was reprinted in *Fieralingue — Health & Illness Anthology*; "Green Olives with Medjool Dates" was reprinted in *Eat This Poem.*

Contents

I

The Body, A Tree	5
Effect	6
Lures	7
Garlic	8
Purity	9
Awake, Midnight	10
Miramar	11
On Living 366 Miles Apart	12
Between Two Ranges	13
Painting the Room I Now Use for Guests	14
Insomnia	15
If You Write a Love Letter to Disappointment	16
Green Olives with Medjool Dates	17
Morning, and the squirrels	18

II

The Body, Before Winter Solstice	21
Turn	22
Early Frost This Year	23
November, Late	24
Through the Window	25
The Body, In Exhaustion	26
First	27
Up	28
We Talk of the Dead	29
Fissures	30
Summer in Ashland	31
The Daylight is Huge	32
Looking for an Oracle	33
Afternoon Storming	34
The Body, In Pain	35
Kintsukuroi	36
Murmur	37

The Drain	38
It Takes a Few Days	39
Thinning	40
What I Know For Sure	42
Under	43
Castellation	44

III

The Body, In Summer	49
New	50
Lusting	51
Ten Minutes Left	52
Ritual	53
How You	54
Before You Kissed Me	55
Poem Written on Valentine's Day	56
The Day We Both Call In	57
A Kiss on the Cheek	58
Heat and Hunger	59
We Talked for Eight Hours Straight Once	60
Telegram	61
I Close My Eyes When I Listen to Poetry	62
About the Author	63

Many of these poems are autobiographical, and some of them are persona (or just out and out fiction). I hope, all together, they tell a story.

To my Saturday, Sunday, and from-afar workshop-mates: Some of you I'm with, some of you are scattered, and all of you I remember. Thank you, thank you for the impact you've had on my work. (And many thanks, as always, for simply putting up with me.)

THE BODY, A TREE

AMY MacLENNAN

I

The Body, A Tree

might think itself lemon,
overgrown behind a steel-grey house,
and pulls in fat bees,
holds to bright and sour.
Or imagines itself almond,
squirrels crazing through branches,
cracking furred hulls,
a chattering, all limbs. But
maybe apricot,
sap almost glowing
on rough bark,
with leaves to drop, shine, wither
on grass. The body wishes.
For soil, for fruit.
For light to grow through,
wood hardening
to an ache.

Effect

Two in the morning, soft scrub of his beard
grazing my lower back and I, half-asleep,
think of a breeze across fielded wheat. I think
of effect. Our bodies, marked many times over,
faded gash on his left shoulder,
glossy stitched line beneath my chin,
have learned this on their own.
I will sleep soon, and the pillow
may leave a crease on my cheek —
in the morning, I won't even know it's there.

Lures

It happened three times,
my dangle earring hooked
to your beard, a clean
catch.
      I've changed
to hoops now,
we come away
without a snag.
           And still
I feel the pull: my face
tugged back to yours,
a line between us
tight.

Garlic

Four more cloves crushed into hummus,
spread on toast, a mashing
so thick with garlic it almost pollutes us,
hangs on our air, our tongues pickled
though I kiss you and can't sense it in your mouth,
just my own, and the sting stays
until we sleep and my sweat runs with it then,
spilling into the quilt, spicing the feathers,
and in such a stew I dream of my hair
curling out to my feet, of your eyes
changing color again, I fall into snow
and melt it down to slush, orange birds
fly from between my legs and I smell
mango, coconut, until I jerk awake,
my body damp, a mist still in my eyes,
knowing nothing but my craving for sugar
and the taste I know of you.

Purity

We spoon up honey, a single-blossom strain,
to taste for eucalyptus, find only
sweetness. When you close your eyes,
groping for purity,
I can feel the air of you, I am that raw.

Awake, Midnight

Awake, midnight,
a throb of crickets
pours through each window,
sound that takes the weight of me.

Miramar

We walk the same strip each time,
long stretch of beach
between the weather-beaten house
with high windows
and an outcrop of rock, the place
tides creep and lick
the cliff's base. Always this seascape, landscape —
your eyes scanning
water, across seals, buoys, small boats,
while I look to our feet,
our sneakers plowing through shell shards
smoothed out and glossed,
ribbons of kelp, driftwood bits all splits
and holes. We don't talk
above the water-crash, we just walk our patch
of sand, hair whipping
our faces and stinging our eyes, we keep
to our elements as the sun
cants down in the same slice of sky. We have done
this four times, twelve times,
twenty-six. We think we'll do it again. Same shore,
same sun, same shells.
And the tide goes out as we turn from the coast,
beach face running
with foam and trails of receding sand.

On Living 366 Miles Apart

You say, *Don't take it so hard*.
You say, *Be positive*.
And I take each day

like a matchstick struck
then flung to an iced sidewalk,
flamed to black smudge.

The cats crouch in high windows
now. They watch. As I watch
winter's last geese feeding

in the field's browned grass.
I say, *I miss you*.
I say, *I'll try*.

We spend our weathers
apart. For you, it's metronome rain.
For me, the wind won't stop.

And the sugar won't take
to the tea anymore. I swear,
I swallow cold grains whole.

Between Two Ranges

It's where you think you'll stop —
a smallish town. Houses with porches
that seem like promise.
The two of you will cruise through
in an afternoon, and the café
will serve coffee sweet with hot milk.
The chairs feel familiar, the tables
impossibly smooth. Floors
will creak like home. When you walk back
to the truck, you'll see a single hawk
on a light post and say, "Luck."
And firs on a mountain ridge
with silhouettes of couples dancing:
you imagine they'll never change.

Painting the Room I Now Use for Guests

The colors are endless. Small papers
with green done forty-five ways.
I need to change my ex-lover's
office, cover his nail holes,
paint over the breath-steeped walls.
I hunt for a color to blanket
the yellow once plain but now
weak and pallid. My colors
have gone sour, past-laden,
memory-smacked. Coral shoes now hum
with jealousy, plum of pillowcases
drenched with regret. But the white
threading my hair is still mine,
the sun-bleached rug, the tarnished
silver frame. I'll paint that room
a soft gray, will wait for my colors
to come back. One day I could see
the tangerine vases perched on my shelves,
how they glow bright as desire,
how they might murmur *forget*.

Insomnia

Three a.m. always smothers you deep.
Dull glow of numbers on the nightstand
and sweat running down your ribs.
These nights are cello suites, unbloomed tulips,
weed-clogged creeks. You might reach
for something to hold, a small rock shard
or seashell piece, and think you might worry out
all the edges, imperfections. You go to the fridge
for cold water, stand in the inevitable light,
see green olives, peach jam,
and the lettuce, wilted, semi-strewn
as a dress balled up on a stranger's floor.

If You Write a Love Letter to Disappointment

Allow brevity. Allow sweetness.
Allow smudged ink.
Do not use exclamation points.
Do not speak in the third person.
Bring your best paper. Tolerate
the passage of time. You may
drink water. Try not to drink wine.
Write alone, but imagine
others in the room.
Use adjectives if you like,
and end sentences with prepositions.
Do not repeat yourself. Invite
generosity, permit humor.
Avoid sarcasm, but accept grief.
Draft the letter as if
you could only write it once.
Use a long salutation
and a short goodbye.

Green Olives with Medjool Dates

Sweetness to take the tang
from the salt. Similar opposites.
Like *built* and *guilt* — one high, one low.
As when your life
strips you down: you look up.
Even when it all
stings deep, a memory
of sugar in your mouth.

Morning, and the squirrels

Morning, and the squirrels
squeak-chuff in the trees —
my waking so clean,
I am the air.

II

The Body, Before Winter Solstice

now almost fading, amaryllis
too far from windows
leaning toward any sunned
slant. The body yoked
by *starve* and *crave*
from a feeding of milk
by the dropper
when it would gulp
it down fast by the cup.
The body, before solstice,
knows the unspooling
will come soon,
sheets untwisting at dawn,
but the hours pass only
as cranberries grow,
even as there's a begging
for the spill of cherries
across the fingers,
the mouth.

Turn

The air is turning today. Even
with scorching weeks,
a month of summer ahead,
a skeletal-tree wind slings
early winter on an August afternoon.
Across browned grasses
it blows *surrender*. It blows *forget*.
I button my coat,
wipe dust from my stinging eyes,
a season thrown full across my reluctant back.

Early Frost This Year

And now the first drive
through freezing fog
that seems like it might hang
until March, sunrises placed
somewhere else.
The shower that morning,
lights in the bathroom
just burned out, the one bulb left
soft through the steamed curtain.
This is the fading time,
the smothering time —
return of sallow faces,
heavy clothes all grays and blacks,
start of moods to eclipse.
This is the morning to take
a violent breath,
a gathering of anything green
or wilt-free left.
A token for the waiting,
flood in the lungs, a push
through our fallow sink and hush.

November, Late

For my mother

The rains arrive. They'll stick
until next May. Time now
for cold bathroom floors, damp entryways,
the dry hack. Ends of day sliced down,
the trees just seem to shake.
And I wait.
    Before she died,
I gave her flowers (a wash of roses)
or sweets. Candies, toffee, fudge.
Things of the moment. Nothing
that lasted. Her language fading away,
she called when she got a bouquet.
Two yellows, one white, three reds,
a pink, a yellow, a red…
Lost count. Forgot.
Started over.
    And the wet leaves
stick to my porch, my steps.
Slick, they soak a shape shadow
to the cement. Each day shifts the pattern.
And the rain washes.
    Her favorite
was the raspberry creams. Dark chocolate
and smooth pink center. She'd bite,
chew slowly, finish one off. Carefully
crumple the wrapper. Look into the box
for another.
    Daylight will come back
with new leaf folds on the tips
of branches. I watch for them
even now, even as the dying ones remain.

Through the Window

A feeding robin,
flighting V of geese,
then oaks tossing leaves
to the failing grass.
Follow the sketched line
of thronged hills north,
watch as your breath hazes
the double-paned glass.
Imagine the window shattering
then think of how
it might always hold tight.
A squirrel starts
its run to the field,
and a wind sends the oaks'
offerings to cartwheel,
break, then settle and wait.

The Body, In Exhaustion

now a rusted swing set,
browned chains, cracked plastic,
moan of metal
in November wind.
Even asleep, the body tears itself
in dream, hands flustering
through sheets, disintegrating
the cotton thread by thread.
The body, in exhaustion,
might feast on itself,
imagine pearls of maggots
to curl and suck, eke just enough,
but remembering
the pail of butter,
full and sweet,
the melting
slow and long
and ago.

First

Late March, a mountain,
and snow slips from fir boughs,
throws shadows like birds plunging to earth.

Ebb time. Stark trees
furred in sharp green,
lupine poppy haze low on the hills.

Freak spring, false
summer, days of blast,
glare, blossom hail in the streets.

And some mornings
still come crisp, break hard
with frost. Glinting and imperfect birth.

Up

Most times the alarm cuts through,
high tones that jerk me
to sudden morning. It takes a weekend
for honest waking, the swim up
through a wild league of ocean,
last breath of sleep to carry me
from the reaches, ears ringing, just
a blur left from the quieting city below.

We Talk of the Dead

It's a subject that comes up, often. Dead friends,
dying wives, a brother breathing out his days
from lungs shriveled to rot. We say
they'll see a light or their lives will flip
like a picture book left on some breezed beach.
We talk of ease. But what if,
in that gloaming, they see ahead?
And the flash is not of them, but us?
They'll know our choked words, our food
on small tables. They might see the mist
that drips down our windows
and the crumbs on the floor. And they will see
when we begin to sweep and fold clothes,
when we ink names on birthday cards
and lick the flap closed. They'll know
the running starts we take and when
we finally sit still in boredom.
They might see everyone in the life once theirs,
they'll feel the rattle of many doors,
and if they look at us, in the final flow
of blood, their eyes might say,
it's okay, you'll see soon enough,
you, too, will see it all.

Fissures

Eight in three days,
these headaches. My doctor
calls them clusters, but to me
they're swarms, like earthquakes,
rocking my skull, slipping its tilt.
A nuisance, yes, to drag out
the compresses and pain killers
as I log the times, chart the run.
And a darkened room
can't always be found in a pinch.
But I worry more about a shift,
the trifling cracks
and splits in my brain
bleeding toward a break. I try
to bypass stress, but this world fairly
throbs. I can only stock up
on bland soup, herb tea
and keep my address
on a tag around my wrist —
who knows where I'll be
when the big one hits.

Summer in Ashland

I breathe
smoke from stewing fires,

eight hundred or so at last count,
dry lightning strikes snapping
statewide, late spring grass
turned kindling pouch,

and it burns, all burning,
acres enraged, the valley a chimney
churning a state's worth of murk,

gray haze smudging the sky,
no clouds now, and I suck in
particulate — weed, tree,
house ash, pull in the evening gloom,

watch the day give in
with a sulfur honey sun.

The Daylight is Huge

The daylight is huge.
Five a.m. and the sky already
blushing gray. Mornings so full
of blue the clouds almost sheepish
as they wisp over hills.
High noon only happens in June,
mid-day a tipping point, the scale
weighed down on both sides
with blazed hours. And the evenings —
so drawn out the land lies stunned
by that shambling last light.

Looking for an Oracle

Spool it on out for me: where to turn left,
the bananas to pick, the men to catch,
the men to ditch, tell me when my nails
will break and the roof will fail,
tip me to gossips and scratched-out phone book names,
list out my losses (hearing gone in ten years,
the loves I'll bury),
line them up so I can swallow them all
without the coil of worry —
choice never stopped the clots in anyone's veins
or the smooth sky pressing down,
and I want my days laid flat,
my facts splayed out, a plan, a map,
to the last damn chicken bone
that sticks in my throat.

Afternoon Storming

Late August, flat heat, and the sky
almost scrapes her clouded belly
across the mountain ridge. Still and still,
one vast hush, hum in the air,
balled-up time waiting for
                              that distant glint,
and the air finally lives, flare and boom,
a hurly-burly jig shaking its way
across the valley floor — fuss, heavage,
blinks and streaks, low bellowed tones,
long calls to another snap of light —
it's all pell-mell, flurry of drops,
                              teeming sweat,
the work of it all, flash, din,
steam rising from soil, green exhaustion,
fury, glory, the sighs and light,
sulky girl slamming the door.

The Body, In Pain

plank of the long pang,
stubborn continent, locked,
ready to heave, a quake,
sinkhole spasm. The body, in pain,
can twitch at the rub
of linen or flinch when forced
to twist a knob or lid,
and it may lie
listless, become its own bed.
The body, in pain, might not
even fumble for ease,
just hang from a hard-barked tree
while branches creak
something like a song,
slow, wind-driven, low.

Kintsukuroi

The art of repairing pottery with gold or silver.
For Stephen Sadler

Imagine the bowl
on a table cupping
late-summer fruit.
Think of the tip or knock
and pottery once whole
now in shards. It could be
five pieces, nine, fourteen.
The bowl breaks differently
with any given drop.
This time silver patterns
the seams like long slick rivers
instead of the jags
of a mountain ridge.
Imagine our bodies, the shine
of ten-year-old scars,
knobs of re-set bones.
Think of the way we fill
our crumbling teeth
and hold our own gold.
We piece our fragments together
a new way each time,
we repair what we can.
Our vessels holding blood
and bone make a changed shape,
and we long to be more gorgeous
with the breakage.

Murmur

I never thought about it, not
in a physical way.
I'm young, my health sound.
This heart slogged on,
and I only made mention
(in the breaking sense)
after my father's final stroke
or when a good love left.
Now I pay attention —
my heart murmurs.
Murmur.
A sexy name for a leak.
One doctor said she heard
a *ssshhh*. The other,
a snapping second beat.
Call it prolapse, call it
floppy valve. I think of it
as a whisper,
a stream of secrets
hissing in my breast.
Listen. Listen.

The Drain

For my mother

I don't know what to say when you
come home. It's gone and you're left
with a bandage wrapped
around your chest.
I heat soup for supper, complain
about the line-up on TV until
it's time to change your drain.
You ask if I'd like to watch. I do;
I want to see.   Pinned to thin strips
of gauze, the plastic bottle trails
a tube that snakes its way
under your arm, the pieces
translucent, almost graceful.
No more than this to let
your closed wound weep.
                              You do it
without a hitch: pour the fluid out,
check the tube, zip your top. And when
you're done, you seem pleased,
and I say I'll slip something
into that flask, a goldfish,
a gummy bear. You laugh
as you get ready for bed.
A locket, two frosted red dice.
And we giggle as you pull
the blanket up. A chess piece maybe,
a key.

It Takes a Few Days

She shops. Blue bands
to tie her hair back.
Nail clippers, sweatshirts,
socks. Two bars of Ivory.

The housework. She scrubs
with dutch cleanser,
no gloves. The bathtub almost
radiant. Even the drain.

A guy strips the board
from her window, replaces
it with glass so pure
everything can be seen.

She double checks her spelling
in the emails she answers.
Shared, not *shard*. *Care*, not *came*.
She's always had trouble with *beautiful*.

Thinning

Her morning meal, no more
smoothies of grapefruit,
protein powder, kelp —
she gagged on the flavor,
the feel in her mouth,
but choked more
on herself, squishy
thighs, belly spilling over
ever tighter jeans
already two sizes up.
Her breasts puffed
as well, but the cleavage
felt almost obscene, not
sexy but a sign
her body wanted
to envelop itself.
So her morning starts
with two cups
of coffee, two smokes,
two shots. Muddled
at first, but
her weight drops,
a hot air balloon
settling, a slack
collapse. So two
became three,
woozy and craving
became one. Her smell
changes from an earthy
musk to a sharp
smell of grass just
starting to decay.

She trades in lunch
too, it works, it all
works, brings her back
to bones showing
under skin. She
figures a few months,
enough to feel a new
self, to be
a compost heap,
slow rot to shrink
her down until
she filters all
that is wrong.
She tries hard
to remember slight
breezes against the hair on
her arms, the languish
of a slow pulse. She
no longer thinks
of the taste
of fresh-baked bread
or cantaloupe.

What I Know For Sure

with thanks to Deborah Kennan and page 48

Regret melts only to shape itself.
Pillar candle wax
hot-pooling to a mock lake —
thin light, waiting burn,
liquid cup brimming
to spill, harden, brittle,
sweet mess always
blurring something,
anything, everything
in the end. It took
a lot to love you.

Under

They're banished to under the bed.
Papers from my mother's estate,
photos of loves that left,
my grandmother's costume jewelry
she always said was real.
High school yearbooks (my hair
a mess) on top of the cheap taffeta
still torn and stained with cheap red
from after the prom. I imagine
throwing it all out, chucking
the boxes whole, intact, or
I could sort it all out —
what necessary (tax audit),
what not. I'll see
if I peek. I only touch them
when I move, new dust smudges
in place of the old. All I know
is removing them won't help.
They've always been there,
I'll see them anyway, breathe in
the paper, cloth, metal, wood.
All I can do is press my weight down,
keep the cartons closed,
smother them with my sleep.

Castellation

Engineering term: having indentations similar to battlements

On the workbench,
grimed up, slightly rusted,
a chunk of carved-out metal
the size of a child's hand.
Doughnut-shaped and jagged,
I pick it up, trace
the greek key lines,
see the threads inside,
a nut for a very big bolt.
I ask my friend
what it is.
A castellated nut, he says,
used on very old cars,
something to keep
a vibrating screw in place.
But you can't overturn,
underturn it, you
have to twist and lock,
get that turn just right.
I've come over
to have coffee,
a bit tight myself,
after a long call
with my lover,
wait, ex-lover,
about how
we'll sort things out,
who gets what,
the cell phone minutes,
cheese knives,

big screen TV. We were
careful, not too harsh,
not too delicate.
Of course, now,
I think of us
as bolt to nut,
the care we'd taken
to grease our pairing.
We did not mean
to strip our threads.
But it was a jarring ride,
a hard shaking,
our metals broke,
tore our castle apart.

III

The Body, In Summer

with sinews all syrup
and skin sweat-licked,
seems always
out-facing, unfurled,
slow spasm of *open* and *want*,
even hair more eager,
twisting out fast
to bleach and hold
July light. The body,
in summer, now a boat,
small sway in water,
a float of belly and back
as it craves melon, tomato,
corn warm from the field,
and the body knows well
the length of the day,
tries to think only
of coral skies and sure desire,
long peal of the naked, evening sun.

New

Dip of your collarbone,
slant of your thigh, the dusting
of moles on your upper arm.
I chart you slow.
Expanse of your back,
stepping stones of spine,
how your edges blend
under flesh. Your wristbones
slide under my fingers,
a different combination; your hands
in mine, a different lock.
The sheen on your skin
almost reflects me. My fingertips
graze your beard, and I try to imprint
the stubble below your lip.
Your smell is like a new mineral,
your taste bright like pink salt.
You are my just-opened trunk,
tree-top perch, high desert,
cupboard of spices, spring-planted garden.
My favored foreign land.

Lusting

It starts with your walk
across the plaza, your orange fleece coat
a dull glow in the day gone dusk.
It ends with you arms around me,
your handprints almost marking my clothes,
staining my back.

It starts with the glass of wine
that turns into three, cabernet
that makes me thirst and thirst.
It ends with the taste in my mouth,
how I remember yours
bright with wine still on your tongue.

It starts with your eyes, the old cliché,
but your hazels don't sparkle,
they crackle, they smoke, small bonfires.
It ends with an itch, thistleburr tingle
in my thighs, how I shift in my chair,
how my skirt inches up.

It starts with your face near mine,
your nose just grazing my cheek,
your breath an impossible touch.
It ends with our walk to the car,
the way we say nothing, the drive to your bed,
how I know, hours from now, sheets will settle on our skin.

Ten Minutes Left

maybe fifteen, before driving to work, surrendering
the warmth of you. You run
the tips of my nails, I scan each groove
of your joints, both of us eyes closed,
the clock's tick soft, inevitable. At first,
your hand the moon's surface,
all texture, surprising, expansive.
Time creased hard there, each callous a story,
ends of your fingers like glass.
Then what I feel, your movement,
like the licking of the sea, searching,
gentle questions, all slow pull,
almost a current on my skin.
We're final clicks away, and I sense
just bones now, dip and rise of each knuckle,
hard edges of your wrist. I memorize this.
I could leave your bed now,
leave you for years, two, seventeen, forty.
And one day, in any darkness, if our hands meet,
I will know you.

Ritual

Top sheet first,
tugged up to pillows,
goose-downed, mashed,
and they're next in line
for plumping and placing,
our heads just here,
my pillow sideways,
yours still with a curl
of my hair coiled
into the threads.
The comforter now
with two or three shakes,
cotton on cotton,
fibers frictioned
across each other
one last time.
And now the bed waits
like I wait
to unbuild our bed again,
strip it apart,
toss it into a mess
of longing and night.

How You

take from my plate at parties,
kalamatas and red flame grapes,
bring back soft cheeses and dates,
together you say.
                    laugh when I catch my hair
in earrings, a necklace,
your sunglass frames, you say
you've never seen me
without something curling.
                        and never brush
left-behind wisps from our sheets, you say
it would be like taking a bit of me away,
and how you say
           please soap my back,
the stretch of spine
just out of reach.
                you say you'd have your mouth
on me everywhere, want mine
to pass all across you,
              how you know
the soft salt where each of my fingers meets
my hand, how you know it
without even tasting.

Before You Kissed Me

My hand felt it first
in that wisp of time
when our fingers slid
on a well-worn blanket,
my skin a white flush
as your flesh came close —
the moment of frantic burn
when I imagined our noses
settling to each other's cheeks,
tip of my tongue across
the slick edge of your teeth.

Poem Written on Valentine's Day

Our trail to the bed tangles —
slippers, lace-up shoes,
your shirt still half-buttoned,
my coral blouse peeled,
jeans slithered from both of us,
panties, boxers MIA,
someone's slack belt
under a sheet, the pillow
jabbed with my barrette,
a bra — I won't remember
if I wore one...
                    and once in bed,
we unravel then knot,
re-adorn each other,
one unblushing
bit of skin at a time.

The Day We Both Call In

Of course, we intend to get up,
shed ourselves from each other,
all warmth and buttery skin,
but we're coiled, your belly
to my back, five more minutes,
your arm a honeyed weight,
I kiss your palm, ten more
minutes, I imagine your hands
covered in oil, every speck
of me slicked, we'll be late,
the hush of May rain
soaks our quilt, our heads dazed
with pillows, and we know now
I'll have a migraine,
you'll have the flu…
we're sick, unable to shake
what makes us sweat
and tremble and ache.

A Kiss on the Cheek

It seems chaste enough,
a pursed-lip tap.
                But with some,
your mouths
                so near, you know
how close you really are.
A gradual lean,
pause,
      just an inch away,
he feels your breath,
                a wait,
and with the bow of your lips
you place
        a tiny glare
of hold and sway
to his face
           then you pull back,
again the wait,
           the kiss
flushing there,
your slight
        sigh
now lighting it up,
and with
        a tongue flick
to the spot you just left,
it's now
        a keepsake,
favorite stain,
              languished smoke mark,
a hushed
        invitation for
soon.

Heat and Hunger

You kiss the top of one shoulder,
a run of your lips across the strip
where my bra strap hits.
I trace circles at the place
your fingers meet your hand,
stroke the mild webbing there.
A dainty scorching
of each other's skin,
such a delicate devouring.

We Talked for Eight Hours Straight Once

In bed, a Saturday morning
a molasses of lovemaking,
we poured ourselves on to each other
then in. Slow, lazy,
like we'd never been solid.
Then we talked. About what
I can't recall, but you
were still syrup on my skin.
About our exes probably, our jobs.
We didn't eat, I felt full
the whole time. We were still
melting through each other.
Not even a glass of water.
I remember how the sheet
draped across our legs.
It was a pure spring day,
we planned a late morning hike,
but we stuck to bed,
didn't leave it once.
We probably talked
about our fathers, maybe
our Christmases as kids.
We didn't even realize
it was past noon,
still planning to go out.
We had eased and mellowed
to our pillows, a light blanket
slipped almost to the floor.
I remember it was April.
I remember how I felt sticky for hours,
how that day was a drowsy,
sleepless night.

Telegram

After, we sprawl. Our arms looped,
my foot against your calf, your hand
on my thigh, a completed circuit,
uncomplicated. As we drift, your fingers
start the nerve spasm of sleep,
morse code tap as you passage,
a message I do not know
how to decipher. I let your dispatch
play through me, chains of letters
that tell everything
you haven't said, so many words
strung together — and I can't
make sense of them.
I am sinking too, into a night
where we turn and settle —
our communiqués in the form of pulse
and slow breath. Before sleep
takes me, I imagine a cable to you,
each word well-chosen, costly...
one of us will leave
I will remember my body
ached for you like no other stop

I Close My Eyes When I Listen to Poetry

People notice. But I still close my eyes
in class, at readings. The table legs,
scarred floors, cups of coffee get in the way,
almost blur the words. Even the light
is too much. I don't want to see you,
poet speaking from the books, poet of the open mike.
Not your fingertip scanning down the page,
not your mouth. I want to be
your mouth, in the dark, your tongue
between our lips, the liquid l's and r's,
a fricative f in that inverted kiss.
I wait for your keening words, your aching words,
first spoken with no one else there, sounds
of animal or infant, fragmented, green,
pawed through and kept. Still naked.
And when you pause, I breathe as you do,
leaning toward the air in your throat,
your projected wanting, your final line.

About the Author

Amy MacLennan sits on the board of Chautauqua Poets & Writers in Ashland, OR. Amy is the Editor of *Cascadia Review,* Managing Editor of *The Cortland Review*, and a poetry editor for *Bone Bouquet*.

Her work has been published in *Cimarron Review*, *Cloudbank*, *Connotation Press*, *Folio*, *Hayden's Ferry Review*, *Linebreak*, *Naugatuck River Review*, *Painted Bride Quarterly*, *Pearl Magazine*, *Pirene's Fountain*, *Poet's Market*, *Rattle*, *River Styx*, *South Dakota Review*, *Spillway*, *The Oregonian*, *The Pedestal Magazine*, *Windfall*, and *Wisconsin Review*.

Amy has published two chapbooks: *Weathering* (Uttered Chaos Press, 2012) and *The Fragile Day* (Spire Press, 2011).

www.ingramcontent.com/pod-product-compliance
Lightning Source LLC
Chambersburg PA
CBHW021450080526
44588CB00009B/778